Having F

By Jenna Lee Gleisner

Picture Glossary

It is fall.

I see clouds.

clouds

It is fall.

I see leaves.

leaves

It is fall.

I see pumpkins.

pumpkins

It is fall.

I see a scarecrow.

scarecrow

It is fall.

I see apples.

apples

It is fall.

I see football.

football

What is on the ground?

clouds

leaves

pumpkins

scarecrow

apples

football